EIGHTH NOTE ♪ PUBLICATIONS

Divertimento No. 1
Allegro con Spirito

Franz Joseph Haydn
Arranged by David Marlatt

The *Allegro con Spirito* movement of the *Divertimento No. 1* in B flat is from the *Six Feldpartiten* (open air suites), composed by Franz Joseph Haydn in the early 1780's. The *Feldpartiten* were discovered by Karl Ferdinand Pohl, librarian for Vienna's Gesellschaft der Musikfreunde, while researching a biography of Haydn. The pieces were composed for the military band of Prince Esternazy of Hungary and were originally scored for two oboes, two French horns, three bassoons, and a B-flat serpent.

ISBN: 9781771579209
CATALOG NUMBER: WWE222190
COST: $15.00
DURATION: 3:00
DIFFICULTY RATING: Medium
2 Flutes, 2 Clarinets

www.enpmusic.com

DIVERTIMENTO No. 1
Allegro con Spirito

F.J. Haydn
(1732-1809)
Arranged by David Marlatt

Flute 1

DIVERTIMENTO No. 1
Allegro con Spirito

F.J. Haydn
(1732-1809)
Arranged by David Marlatt

DIVERTIMENTO No. 1 pg. 2

Flute 2

DIVERTIMENTO No. 1
Allegro con Spirito

F.J. Haydn
(1732-1809)
Arranged by David Marlatt

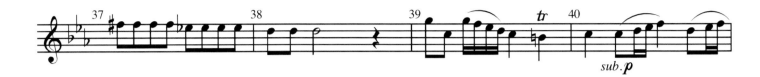

Bb Clarinet 1

DIVERTIMENTO No. 1
Allegro con Spirito

F.J. Haydn
(1732-1809)
Arranged by David Marlatt

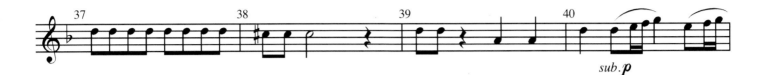

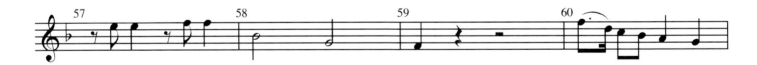

DIVERTIMENTO No. 1
Allegro con Spirito

F.J. Haydn
(1732-1809)
Arranged by David Marlatt

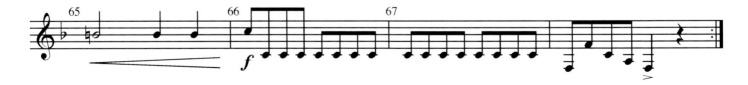

DIVERTIMENTO No. 1 pg. 2

DIVERTIMENTO No. 1 pg. 2

DIVERTIMENTO No. 1 pg. 3